What About Now?

Modern Issues Reflected Back to Their Foundations

TS Taylor

Other Books by TS Taylor

Life-Changing Devotionals

The Love and Mercy of God as Seen in Jonah, Job, and Joseph

Flight to Freedom, Laws to Live By, How to Worship

Exodus Devotionals

High and Lifted Up – Is God Still Engaged in His World?

Isaiah Devotionals

Walk with Jesus and His Followers

Matthew Devotional

Life Applications from Romans

Romans Devotional

Reflections on Faith and Science from Genesis to Current Events

How to Bridge the Gap Between Faith and Science – Small Group Study Book

Luke's Gospel

Eyewitness Account Devotionals

Reflections on Forgiveness

What Does the Bible Tell Us about Forgiveness

What About….?

Interesting Thoughts in the Bible

Reflections on the Psalms – Book 1

Learning to Love God More Deeply

John's Gospel

Who is Jesus? A Devotional

All for the Glory of God

ISBN:979-8-89619-616-7

Cover Photograph: Pixabay - Patjosse

Printed in the United States of America

What About Now?

Modern Issues Reflected Back to Their Foundations

Contents

Other Books by TS Taylor 2

Introduction 1

Who Are the Oppressors and How Can I Become One? 5

If God Does Not Exist, Are All Things Permissible? 10

What Does Sexual Identity Mean? Why Does it Matter? 13

Transgender Children, Who Should Lead?..........................17

Men in Women's Sports. Why Should We Care?....................22

If Climate Change Is Such a Big Deal, Why Do Most People Act Like They Don't Care? 26

What's Wrong With "If It Feels Good, Do It"? 30

How Can the Wealthy and the Poor Better Fit Together? 33

Why Are Babies Important?......................................39

What Is Important in Education Today? 45

Are We Still Evolving, in a Good Way?............................49

What Would Charles Darwin Say About the World Today?...........54

How Can We Better Harness Technology? 59

Why Don't Toilets Clean Themselves? 59

Why Should I Even Care? 63

Concluding Thoughts 68

Prayer to Accept Jesus 69

Acknowledgments 72

Introduction

You may find this reflection guide to be somewhat different from other reflection guides in that its focus is on modern-day problems and how they are reflected back into the past.

You can read and work through this Reflections Book by yourself, but you may find that it is a more helpful study done with a small group of friends. After all, these are difficult societal problems.

As You Read

Feel free to read these reflections in any order that you like. You may want to skip over some, you can also go back to them at another time. Feel free to read at your own pace. It is not intended to be an exhaustive study of modern problems. You may find that you want to do your own independent study of other issues that you think are important today.

Enjoy the questions. They are meant to be open-ended. As such, some of the questions may bring multiple perspectives. If one resonates with you, feel free to ask other deeper questions.

Personal Study or Small Group?

This book can be used for either personal study or with a small group. If you use it with a small group, think about how best to use your time together.

Open Mind. Come with an open heart and mind so that you best honor the time together.

Summarize and discuss. Have one or two people in the group summarize the reflection for this meeting. Ask everyone what they particularly liked (or disliked) about this writing and what was encouraging or challenging.

Questions. Talk through the discussion questions at the end of each reflection. Listen carefully to what others in the group say, as they may be touching on deeper issues. Feel free to allow some questions to take you into a deeper discussion. Also, feel free to table a deeper discussion until another time, to allow those interested to think more about it.

Application. How can you use any of these discussions to have deeper conversations with your friends and neighbors? If you have a specific friend in mind, ask them to read along with you and to reflect on the questions.

For more information join us at:
https://www.tstaylordevotionals.com/

Or connect at:

tstaylor.devotionals@gmail.com

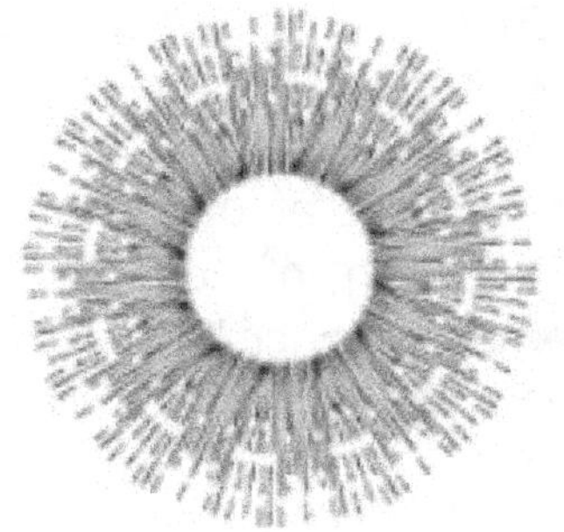

Who Are the Oppressors and How Can I Become One?

Everyone thinks that oppressors are a new political situation in their era, but we have had oppressors since the beginning of time. After all, it goes back to the beginning of time with Cain and Abel.

Now Cain talked with Abel his brother; and it came to pass, when they were in the field, that Cain rose up against Abel his brother and killed him. (Genesis 4:8)

Cain was jealous of his brother Abel and he could not handle it, so Cain killed Abel.

In the 1200s Genghis Khan marched across much of Asia, Russia, and parts of Europe. Genghis Khan was known as a conqueror, or some would call him an oppressor. If your village surrendered willingly, he would just enslave your people and marry off your daughters. If there was a great deal of resistance, he would kill almost everyone, as he did not want prisoners of war. For example, when he invaded Russia, he treated the people very badly. He burned and looted the villages so that he could control the land and the reigning Russian princes. At the peak of his conquests, he controlled a land mass almost the size of Africa. Genghis Khan was a very successful oppressor.

Much later, in 1941, Hitler controlled much of Europe; but compared to Genghis Khan, he controlled many more people, almost 280 million. Why do men, nations, and armies conquer and oppress?

Much of the time it is for natural resources, increased land boundaries, and of course power. Ultimately, power seems to be the overarching reason, for as it has been said "Power tends to corrupt, and absolute power corrupts absolutely."

It seems that as a people, we are addicted to power over others. We all want it, but some of us want it more than others. Some of us try to get it in a backhanded way, by freeing the oppressed. Doing this gives us a measure of power over the rest of the world. Generally, when we feel that we are part of the elite over the oppressed, we want to remain there as we want to be seen as their saviors.

In the 1840s, Karl Marx tried to free up the oppressed. He saw oppression coming from work and fundamentally by those who controlled the tools of production. The oppressors tried to use religion to dominate the oppressed. The bourgeoisie said that everything would be better for the proletariat in the next life, so they were told to put up with this oppression. As he said, "Religion is the opium of the people." He tried to give more power to the workers, but he never solved the problem of "who would make the next generation production tools?"

How can we make a more balanced life for everyone and not allow power to corrupt us?

This is one of the reasons that Jesus Christ's message was so radical. He said that He can to set people free, all people. To be free they need to accept God's rule.

16 So He came to Nazareth, where He had been brought up. And as His custom was, He went into the synagogue on the Sabbath day, and stood up to read. 17 And He was handed the book of the prophet Isaiah. And when He had opened the book, He found the place where it was written:

18 "The Spirit of the Lord is upon Me,
Because He has anointed Me
To preach the gospel to the poor;
He has sent Me to heal the brokenhearted,
To proclaim liberty to the captives
And recovery of sight to the blind,
To set at liberty those who are oppressed;
19 To proclaim the acceptable year of
the Lord."

20 Then He closed the book, and gave it back to the attendant and sat down. And the eyes of all who were in the synagogue were fixed on Him. 21 And He began to say to them, "Today this Scripture is fulfilled in your hearing." (Luke 4:16-21)

He was quoting from the Old Testament Prophet Isaiah from 700 years before His time. Jesus is the one to set people free. It is an interesting paradox, freedom only comes from submission to the highest power, God.

So, how can you become an oppressor? Perhaps you do not want to become one, for if you do you will die addicted to trying to get more and more power and yet, never having enough. Perhaps you need to submit to a higher power.

Discussion Questions

1. Do you think that everyone wants to become an oppressor, if not the entire world, at least their own personal world?

2. Do you think that "Power tends to corrupt, and absolute power corrupts absolutely"? Can you cite some other examples?

3. What could be done today to limit the "absolute power" of the world's political leaders?

4. What do you think about Jesus proclaiming liberty to the captives?

If God Does Not Exist, Are All Things Permissible?

The famous Russian author, Fyodor Dostoyevsky wrote, "If there is no God, then all is permitted" in 1880 in his book *"The Brothers Karamazov."* What was he getting at with this statement?

Let's assume for a minute that God does not exist. Remember, whether you or I think that God exists, has nothing to do with His existence. He either exists or doesn't exist, and that is outside of our thoughts and views.

If God does not exist there, then there is no Creator or Intelligent Designer behind the universe. Charles Darwin's theory of macroevolution, the idea that we all came from a random combination of amino acids long ago, would win the day. Unfortunately, randomly combined amino acids know nothing of society, art, beauty, morality, or contemplation of big questions like "Why am I here?". Therefore, the random throwing of paint on a canvas should be seen as the same as the great works, such as the Mona Lisa. For some of us, this would be very disappointing.

If God does not exist, there is no basis for morality. Again, Darwin would win the day with the idea that the strongest and those best able to change should survive. Society would collapse to being ruled by the elite, the strongest and most powerful. The only purpose of the rest of society would be to serve the strong elite class. But to what purpose? Perhaps for the purpose of their hedonistic pleasure.

The great French existential thinker, Jean-Paul Satre understood life without the existence of God. Satre lived through WWII and he wrote a great deal after the war. Perhaps that is why his most famous quote is thought to be: "Man is a useless passion. It is meaningless that we live and it is meaningless that we die." He understood that everyone is "born without reason, prolongs itself out of weakness, and dies by chance. If you are lonely when you're alone, you are in bad company. Freedom is what you do with what's been done to you."

Satre understood the consequence of the no God to be a meaningless life, driven by chance, and leading to only meaninglessness. Life is just empty meaninglessness.

This is why the question of God's existence is so important to us individually and as a society.

Discussion Questions

1. If God does not exist, is there anything that is NOT permissible? What and why do you think this?

2. If God does not exist, can there be any art that is better than any other art? If so, what kind and why?

3. Do you think that insects contemplate the origins of the universe and their place in it? Why or why not?

4. How would you go about digging into whether God exists or not?

What Does Sexual Identity Mean?
Why Does it Matter?

For thousands of years sex and gender were very clear to everyone. Sex is and has always been a biological concept that refers to a person's physical characteristics such as reproductive organs or chromosomes.

Gender, as differentiated from sex, is a very modern idea. It is a social construct that refers to a person's self-representation and how they are perceived by society. It allows people to identify with different sexes, races, or cultures.

While the ancient Greeks; Socrates, Plato, and Aristotle debated many ideas and questions, they did not debate sex, gender, and identity.

Plato's Theory of Forms asserted that the physical realm, our reproductive organs as an example, are only a shadow of the true reality in the Realm of Forms. The Realms of Forms is outside ourselves. It gives us a basis of what things really are, and what is true. The Realm of Forms would contain the ideal or perfect concept of physical objects such as sexual organs.

One way of looking at the modern idea is that we have moved Plato's Realm of Forms from the external perfect world, transcending time and space, into our minds. With this movement, we can see that we are not a perfect male or female person, but a poor representation of one. We can identify as a person different from our physical characteristics and this allows us to project a different Form from the Realm onto ourselves and hence make us into a different person.

Plato would be very surprised by the idea of moving the Realm of Forms (perfection) into each person's mind and imagination. This would move the idea of one perfect idea or representation of an object to an infinite number of perfect ideas or representations. He would postulate that if there are an infinite number ideas then the ideal does not exist.

Another area to understand in Plato's view on reality is the theater. Plato had a dim view of the theater for several reasons. One was the theater played to people's fantasies and sympathies; therefore, the theater did not help people deal with reality and society's difficulties. Another reason for the Greek's displeasure with the theater is that the actor was a hypocrite. For the Greek word for actor is *hypokrite.* The actors would pretend to be one or several different people in the play so that they would be perceived to be someone they were not. If they were a good actor, they would identify with the character they were playing. But when the play was over, they would have to return to being who they really were.

Plato might think that there is an awful lot of play-acting going on in modern society with people identifying as different people than they were a year ago or five years ago.

Perhaps the ancient Greeks would ask us to move the ideals; what is good, right, and beautiful, outside of ourselves and back into an external Realm of Forms. Perhaps then we could see who we really are.

Discussion Questions

1. What do you think of the idea of the Realm of Forms being outside of ourselves? Does this make any sense today?

2. If the Realm of Forms is outside of us, where is it? How could we get to know it?

3. Do you think that we are all play actors? Why or why not?

4. How can we figure out who we were created to be?

16

Transgender Children, Who Should Lead?

Transgender children are a fairly new social idea. What are not new ideas are that children are different than adults and that children cannot make as informed decisions as most adults. For hundreds and hundreds of years, humanity has believed that children are different from adults and should be protected by the adults who "know more." But, do adults really know more, and if so, what do they really know about?

This takes us back to some of the great debates in the Enlightenment period (late 1600s). Philosophers like John Locke believed that all human knowledge came from our senses; touch, sight, hearing, smell, and taste. Therefore; all human understanding comes from our interpretation and reflection on the input from these physical senses. He also argued that infants did not "know anything" and that they had to learn by interacting with the world around them.

Over the years his ideas have been expanded upon in various ways. One way was the educational system for children. When possible, we found that if we grouped children by age or stage of development, they could learn more and faster as the information fit into their world more appropriately.

We also found that having young children work in hard labor situations, such as a mine or a factory, was detrimental to their physical and mental development. While it took a long time to come to agreement on this, starting in the early 1900s the United States began to enact labor laws that protected children. Perhaps surprisingly, one of the instruments that helped swing public opinion was the camera. People like Lewis Helm began taking photographs of the working conditions for some of these children and the physical injuries that sometimes occurred to these young children. These photographic images, taken in the early 1900s, of children being damaged for life, struck a chord with the empirically minded society as they finally saw the damage with their own eyes. They saw children with damaged hands, arms, or eyes.

Labor laws finally came into the United States in 1938. We all agreed that children were to be protected and given time to develop without life-changing events taking place in their lives or their bodies.

Today, in the United States, one does not become a legal adult until the age of eighteen. While one can work before they turn eighteen, there are still jobs for which they are forbidden, such as: roofing, driving, explosives, demotion, and handling radioactive material.

Not only is there work that they cannot do, but there are also things that they cannot legally purchase, such as: alcohol, tobacco, e-cigarettes, fireworks, and firearms. One might wonder why these odd age-related laws exist.

This is because, in the early 1900s, science was beginning to understand the brain at a whole new level. The cerebral cortex, the outer layer of the brain, was understood to be responsible for reasoning, decision-making, emotion, intelligence, and personality. While the cerebral cortex develops throughout much of our young life, the brain completes this development around the age of 25. The prefrontal cortex is one of the last parts of the brain to mature and it is thought to be responsible for planning and mature decision making.

These scientific discoveries have led us to make some of the laws concerning minors. As a society, we are concerned that they do not purchase or use products that they are not mature enough to fully understand and to prevent them from making life-altering mistakes before they are mature enough to understand the consequences. After all, we do not want them to blow their feet off with a gun.

This leads us to the science behind transgendering children. We all know that children have great imaginations, and some are more vivid than others. We also know that children love to play-act and pretend, for that is how they begin to make sense of the world around them. We know that sometimes children will extend their imaginative play into the real world, such as pretending to be a pirate while in the grocery store with mom or dad. We view this as a healthy way of growing up and interacting with the world.

Therefore, if our eight-year-old son asks for a peg-leg operation or a hook for a hand, we would most likely deny this. Our reasoning would be that he is not mature enough to make that decision on his own. After all, his prefrontal cortex is not very mature and so his long-term planning and decision-making skills are not very well developed.

Likewise, suppose our eight-year-old son or daughter tried to convince us to allow them to have life-altering sexual organ surgery. In that case, we should think seriously about their prefrontal cortex and its development. Perhaps they have to learn more about themselves and the world around them. Perhaps it is time to let science lead us in our adult decisions about our children once again.

Discussion Questions

1. What kind of decisions do you think children should make on their own? Say, a typical eight-year-old?

2. Should we go back to the one-room school model of education? Why or why not?

3. Should we change some age-related purchasing laws? If so, which one and how?

4. How much say should children have in transgender surgery discussions?

Men in Women's Sports. Why Should We Care?

For hundreds of years, it was understood that biological males are bigger, stronger, and faster than biological females. This generally made men's sports more interesting than women's sports because there is more basketball dunking, football linemen crunching, and face boxing in men's sports compared to women's sports.

The first Woman's Rights Convention was held in 1848 in New York. This led to the ratification of the 19th Amendment to the Constitution in 1920, which gave women the right to vote. In 1972, the United States passed Title IX of the Civil Rights Act which stated "No person in the United States shall, on the basis of sex, be excluded from the participation in, be denied the benefits of, or be subjected to discrimination under any education program or activity receiving Federal financial assistance." This was a huge win for women, especially women's sports that were a part of a university program. Women's sports were to get more benefits in university programs because of Title IX than they previously had.

In the mid-2020s society took an interesting turn. Biological men could identify as women and hence they could participate in women's sports. Some of these biological men found that there was great gain in participating in women's sports. As they were often bigger, stronger, and faster than the biological women, they could win many of the competitions. Some of these victories led to financial gains such as better student grants or scholarships. All was good until the biological women started to complain.

Their argument was based on the very principle of Title IX. Title IX was to make things fairer for women, but they were losing out in these competitions on the "basis of sex."

While the debate still rages in social media and the legal systems, it seems clear what the outcome should be, as there are only two outcomes.

If biological males are allowed to compete in any and all women's sports, a number of biological men will choose to identify as women and compete in any and all women's sports where their superior size, strength, and speed are an advantage. Soon, all women's sports leaders will be filled with biological males. They will typically be biological males who cannot compete at an elite level with other biological males, but they can beat most biological females. Therefore, sports for women will be no more, for there will be few women in them.

The other outcome is that we define men's sports to be for biological males only, and women's sports for biological females only, and have a new category of X-gender athletes who can identify however they like. Anyone could compete in the X category. For a while, this would be very interesting, but unfortunately, it would eventually evolve to be a league for mediocre biological males competing against each other. While people might begin to lose interest in this league, it should still be given a chance to succeed.

Why should we care? Largely because athletic competition is good for us as a society. It helps build character, perseverance, and sometimes teamwork. For those who do not participate, it is fun to watch and to participate vicariously. After all, athletic competition has been a part of society for hundreds of years. For example, think back to the Aztecs as basketball, soccer, and lacrosse may have their roots in Aztec games.

Perhaps it is time to unite around one of the two possible outcomes.

Discussion Questions

1. Do you believe that there are only two possible outcomes to this question? If so, which one do you lean toward?

2. Are there some sports in which we will see biological women competing with biological men? If so, which ones and why?

3. How do you think the proposed X League will play out?

4. If we should do something, when should we start?

If Climate Change Is Such a Big Deal, Why Do Most People Act Like They Don't Care?

The Earth is a very large and complex system. For many, many years people have been trying to predict the weather, from the somewhat famous "Farmer's Almanac", first published in 1792, to modern super-computer weather models. And yet, we still cannot predict the weather very accurately.

In fact, in the 1970s, the climate community was concerned that the Earth was actually cooling too fast! The cause was thought to be from aerosol pollutants in the atmosphere reflecting sunlight away from the Earth. Scientists actually considered adding much more carbon dioxide into the atmosphere to counter this aerosol cooling effect. It is a good thing that they did not do this because the presence of carbon dioxide in the atmosphere can persist for centuries and cause a heating of the Earth. Now, we know that too much carbon dioxide is a problem.

1988 was the watershed year when the global community came together to attempt to address the issue of climate change. Almost forty years later, as the people of Earth, we seem to have made only marginal progress. Why is this?

There are several reasons for our poor progress in taking care of the Earth. One is the idea of inertia. We, as a people group, do not like change. One colloquial definition of progress is "Positive change, which got us here, and that is good enough for me."

We like progress when it is good for us individually and we have trouble seeing progress that is good for others whom we cannot see or relate to. Many times, we will only help out those far away from us when we think it will also help us.

As the Earth is a very large and complex system, small changes have very little effect on the entire system. For example, many of us have trouble seeing how our recycling of one aluminum can helps the problem in a significant way. However, we will do that one act because we think "If everyone did this, we can make a difference." While that is true, we often see our resolve eroded out from under us when recycling gets too hard or inconvenient.

Our resolve gets eroded because we see that by people's actions, they clearly say that they are not interested or required to participate in the fight against climate change. It is for the others, and not for me. This is most clearly seen at important Climate Change Summits. These Summits are for some of the most important thinkers on climate change to come together and discuss the problem. As these Summits are in remote and exotic locations, the leaders choose to fly their private jets to the Summit. Each private produces more than ten times carbon dioxide compared to a commercial jet. The outcome of the Summit is often big changes that will affect our personal lifestyle, but oddly enough it will not affect the Leaders' lifestyle. So, some of us say; "Why bother."

Another reason that we lose our resolve is that we are looking for long-term, generation changes. Many of us cannot conceive of this, nor do we know how to act. Several societies seem to understand generational thinking, but they are few and far between. For example, when the Native Americans were fishing in streams, they would always leave the largest fish and the smallest fish and only keep the middle-sized ones. The thinking was that the largest fish are the biggest and smartest and we should want them to pass along their genes to the next generation. The smallest have yet to grow up, and they should be given a chance to get bigger. The idea was to not take all the fish but to leave some for future generations.

The Japanese business culture sometimes differs from the American business culture. American businesses are often focused on the next month, the next quarter, or perhaps the next year. Japanese business culture will also consider these short time frames, but it is not unusual for them to have 10, 20, or even 100-year business plans. This generational thinking is largely unheard of in American businesses.

If we are going to work on really large system problems, we are going to have to learn to think differently. Are we up for this?

Discussion Questions

1. How important is it to have great weather prediction models? Why or why not?

2. Can you think of an example in your life where you wanted progress to stop right where it is? How would you describe this?

3. Do you think the elite climate change thinkers are doing a good job? Why or why not?

4. What should your community do to address climate change?

What's Wrong With "If It Feels Good, Do It"?

A common phrase with the hippie generation was, "If it feels good, do it." This was the great cry of the sexual and freedom revolution in the 1960s. Young people were tired of feeling oppressed by "The Man"; big corporations, and business entities. They were tired of wars around the world. They wanted to live in a world of peace and love.

In the early 1960s, Timothy Leary taught at Havard University and also experimented significantly with the hallucinogenic drug LSD. He was experimenting with mind-altering states and he is well known for the phrase "Turn On, Tune In, and Drop Out." He was hoping to get us to think and experience the world differently, and then make it a better place.

It was a time of great upheaval and wild and passionate experimentation, but it did not last. Why not?

It seems that much of the time life is made up of eating, sleeping, spending time with friends, and personal enjoyment and growth. Sometimes to accomplish these things, work is required. The work is either required to grow food, perhaps in a commune, or to make money that can be exchanged for food, clothing, or shelter.

During all of this, we need to figure out what is the right thing to do. Do we only do things that feel good at the time? How important is delayed gratification? Do we need to save money, or food, to be used at another time? Where do we want to be in five or ten years? Who do we want to be with five or ten years from now?

These are all deep, searching questions that can greatly affect how we live our lives. Unfortunately, there is a great deal of research that says that happiness does not ultimately come from doing whatever we feel like at any given moment. Delayed gratification is very important for both personal growth, but also societal growth. But it requires a new way of thinking.

If that is true, then there will be times when we should not just do what feels good at that time. But, how do we figure this all out?

Discussion Questions

1. Do we still want to get away from "The Man"? Who is "The Man"? Why do we want to get away?

2. Should we continue experiments, like LSD experiments, in our universities? Why or why not?

3. Why is delayed gratification so hard to learn? What can we do differently to teach our children better about delayed gratification?

4. How can we wrestle with the vision or dream of where we want to be five years from now?

How Can the Wealthy and the Poor Better Fit Together?

The problem of rich and poor has been with us for a long, long time. In almost all civilizations there were rich and poor. So, why is this and what should we do about it?

One of the societal, foundational roots comes from ancient Israel and the Ten Commandments. It is interesting to note that the last three commandments are about living together and how to deal with personal property. They are:

15 "You shall not steal.

16 "You shall not bear false witness against your neighbor.

17 "You shall not covet your neighbor's house; you shall not covet your neighbor's wife, nor his male servant, nor his female servant, nor his ox, nor his donkey, nor anything that is your neighbor's." (Exodus 20:15-17)

The eighth commandment is about stealing. This makes it very clear that someone will have something, typically a physical object, that someone else does not have. The idea of not stealing personal property is foundational to almost all societies. This establishes the idea that something is "mine!". This codifies the concept of personal property and expresses it as a good thing for society.

The ninth command is about lying. There are lots of reasons to lie. It can be to tarnish someone's reputation, to justify that something is yours and not someone else's, or to get away with something that you did, like stealing something from someone else. You usually lie to get either ahead in the world or to get something that is not ours.

The tenth commandment is the most overarching in that it says that you should not covet, that is yearning to possess, something that is not yours, but your neighbor's. The commandment even gives some examples, in case it is not clear.

These foundational commandments adhere to the idea that we can own and keep personal property, which seems to be a good thing because all of us have some things that are near and dear to us.

Thousands of years later, the Apostle Paul wrote to a young church in the city of Thessalonica about work and property.

> *10 For even when we were with you, we commanded you this: If anyone will not work, neither shall he eat. 11 For we hear that there are some who walk among you in a disorderly manner, not working at all, but are busybodies. (2 Thessalonians 3:10-11)*

He is helping this young church community to establish guidelines for work and property. The community was established on the premise that there is a great deal to do to keep a community alive and thriving. Not everyone needs to do the same task, but everyone should do something to help. If they are not willing to help, then they should not share in the bounty of the community, in this case, food. He even uses the term busybody to describe people who bustle about and meddle but do not accomplish anything for the common good.

We get from these foundational principles that are thousands of years old that personal property is okay, maybe even a good thing, and that everyone should be involved (work) towards the common good.

If this is the case, why are there poor people? There can be several reasons why there are poor people.

1. They could have been struck by some natural disaster, like a flood, drought, or storm.
2. It could be a result of oppression either from powerful warlords or from the political systems.
3. It could be that they have taken a vow of poverty so that they can minimize their own dependence on physical things and get more in touch with their spiritual side.
4. It could be because they are lazy or refuse to work.

It would seem that each of these situations should be handled differently. For example, in 2005 there was a terrible hurricane, Katrina, that hit New Orleans and caused widespread destruction. Many people and organizations came to the aid of the individuals there, such as Christian organizations like Samaritan's Purse. Many people gave up their time and physical resources to help those made poor by the natural disaster.

Oppression from warlords or political systems is often handled differently, with the best solutions often being help from other political systems.

The fourth reason is the most difficult. We must always recognize that different people have different skills and abilities. Just because one person only produces half of what another person does, does not necessarily mean that they are not working up to their abilities or are a busybody. However, it might well be that they are a lazy busybody and are interested in only hiding their skills and abilities because it is just easier to not work so hard.

The problem gets even more complicated with political systems come into play. For example, in a democratic republic, like the United States, a large number of poor people could outvote a smaller number of wealthy people and enact a law that the wealthy people must give much of their wealth to the poorer people. Would this be fair? How is this different from stealing?

If there is a system that embraces personal property, there will be some people with more and some with less. How we figure out how to live with this may very well define the quality of our civilization.

Discussion Questions

1. What do you think about stealing? Should there be a law of the land against stealing? Why or why not?

2. Is it fair that someone has more skills, strength, intelligence, or wisdom than you? What should we do about this?

3. What can you do to help people who have been hit by a large natural disaster?

4. How would you handle a person in your community who refuses to work, or just does not work up to their potential?

Why Are Babies Important?

From the beginning of time, babies have been an important part of any society or civilization. After all, the Bible starts out with:

Then God blessed them, and God said to them, "Be fruitful and multiply..." (Genesis 1:28)

In an agricultural society, babies were very important because they became part of the family workforce and they quickly provided more work and food than they consumed, so they were a huge benefit to any farm.

As societies became more urbanized, children were not an important part of the families' economic well-being, and so the birth rates dropped. Babies take a great deal of time, effort, and care. In a society where both the man and the woman were working, childcare became a huge economic and logistic issue. They began to ask, along with George Bailey in the movie *It's a Wonderful Life,* "Why do we have all these kids?"

In China, a country with more than a billion people, they saw that they could not feed their expanding population so in 1980 the government enacted the One-Child Policy. This had a dramatic effect on the overall population, for over a generation, fewer young people were being born to replace the older generations. Unfortunately, this had significant unintended consequences. As can be seen in the graph below, the birth rate dropped significantly from 1980 to 2020.

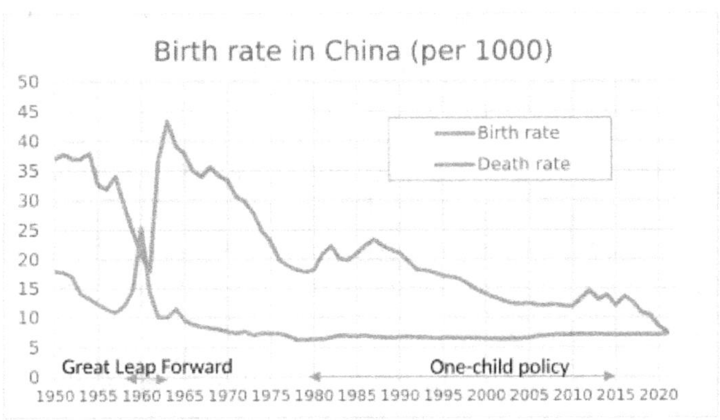

In the 1950's China had a well-balanced agriculturally-based population, as seen in the chart below.

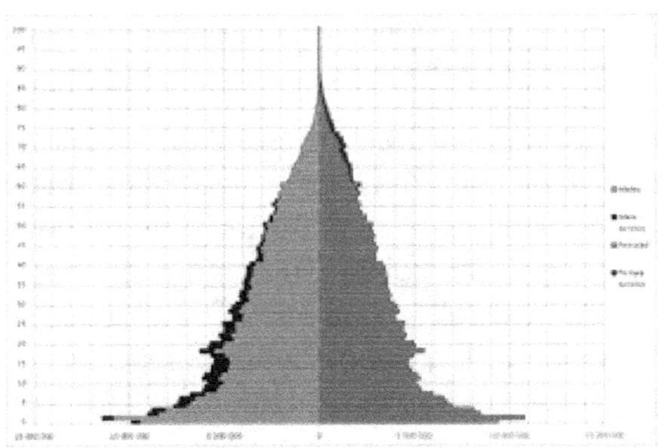

In these graphs, males are on the left, and females are on the right. The ages on the vertical axis are in 5-year increments going from zero to 100 years. This first graph shows many people in the 0 to 10 years old, compared to the working age group, 20 to 50 years old, and many more than in the retired age group, above 60 years old.

Fifty years later, in 2000, twenty years into the one-child policy, there was a significant shift in the population. There are very few 0 to 10-year-olds. While the working ages, 20 to 50 has grown, so has the retired group, those above 60 years old.

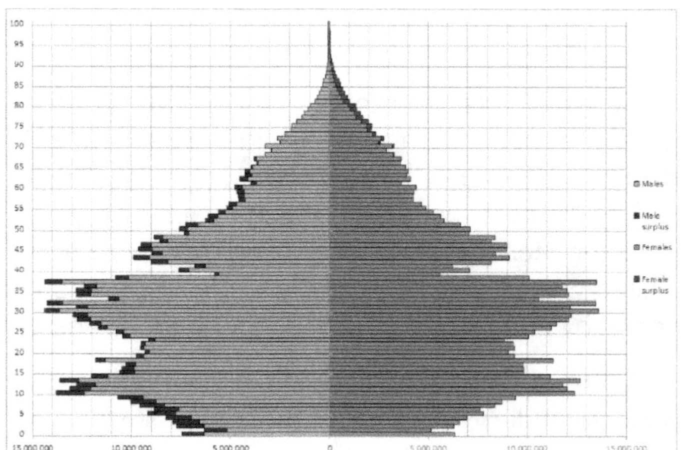

The projected population distribution for 2030 is very dramatic and frightening, as seen below. There are still very few 0 to 10-year-olds. There is also a significant dip in the 20-year-olds, and the retired group is swelling to be bigger than all of the other age groups.

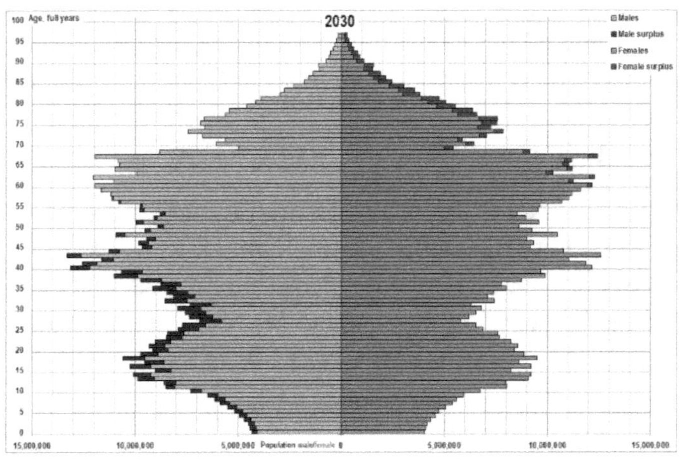

As we all continue to live longer, due to better diets and healthcare, one would wonder "Who is going to take care of all of these older, retired people?" There just aren't enough young people to care for these older people. For example; in the United States, the life expectancy in 1900 was 47 years, by 2000 it had grown to more than 77 years!

There are several possible scenarios for this projected future. One is that the end-of-life care for this huge older, retired age group will come from robotic care. The older generation will be placed in communities where they can be cared for, with little human assistance. Some, especially the elderly, might call this a very dark future.

Another scenario is that euthanasia will be enacted by various governments. These laws will start with reducing the barriers to allowing older people to select their own time and manner of death, to encouraging those who are old or impaired to select their own euthanasia method, to finally requiring those who are in certain physical states or over a certain age to select the euthanasia method. For the elderly, which we will all (hopefully) become, this is also a dark future.

Another hopeful scenario is around the idea that technology in food production and environmental management will advance to state that there is an abundance of food and a well-cared-for environment everywhere. While this is possible, based on our collected history this seems far-fetched.

We have some serious problems ahead of us. One important factor is the birth of babies. Unless we want to have a decreasing population worldwide, we will need to have a total fertility rate of 2.1 to sustain our population. How should we move forward from here?

Discussion Questions

1. Does the significant birth rate, as shown for China, surprise you? Why or why not?

2. Does the projected population distribution for China worry you? Why or why not?

3. What do you think of the possible future scenarios for this population distribution?

4. What do you think we should do with "so many old people"?

What Is Important in Education Today?

Education has been important to societies for a really long time. For example, Socrates is famous for his Socratic Method of teaching. Around 380 BC, Socrates became well known for the method of asking questions as a way of learning. For example, he might ask a student to state their position on a certain policy and then defend that position.

The Greek philosopher Zeno was known for taking philosophical arguments to their logical conclusion. For example, what would happen to the population of China if they enforced a one-child policy forever? If you follow the argument, you will see that they would disappear as a nation, as they could not produce enough people to survive.

For these great Greeks, we see that questioning is important in education. As the world's agricultural societies expanded, we found that education had to work hand-in-hand with farm labor. Therefore, children often worked on the farm early in the morning and then went to a one-room schoolhouse to learn the basics of reading and writing. They needed to learn the skills that would be necessary for the economic growth of the agricultural society. They need to know not only how to grow food, but how to sell it and manage an expanded production.

Then in the late 1700s, the Industrial Revolution started. Life became more about running the factories than working on the family farm. To work in the factories new skills were needed. It was important to be able to sit in one place for a long time and focus on one task. It was important to be on time and to work at the same time as others. Therefore; school bells, rows of desks, and intense focus on a subject became the identifying marks of the educational system.

One would wonder if today we need children who are well-conditioned to sit in one place for a long time or to have their time managed by external bells. Most probably not. As we move to a more technology-assisted and technology-focused society, we will need young people who can work on advanced technology issues as well as how this technology interfaces with the people of society. This could be engineers and programmers, but also artists, UI designers, and urban designers. We will need many people with many skills, all who can work with others with differing skills.

We are quickly finding that our strongly connected technological society with its social media tools, is losing the ability to have people connect with each other on a personal level. Without these personal connections, people are becoming lonely, and sometimes deeply depressed.

We may find that it gets even worse in the future as we bring more and more artificial intelligence tools into teaching and education in general. Will we need more skills or fewer skills, as we have machines that do more of our tasks and thinking?

As AI advances, will there be anything left for us to do that brings us personal meaning?

Perhaps this is where we will see the education system growing, in helping people to find their place in society with their individually focused skills and talents and also to have the ability to talk to each other face-to-face. They will need to find areas of work that bring them meaning and fulfillment. It seems that we have a long way to go in this area.

Discussion Questions

1. What do you think about the Socratic method of teaching by asking lots of questions? Could that work today? Defend your position.

2. Do you think we need school buildings today? Could we do it all with individualized online education? Defend your position.

3. What role should AI play in modern education?

4. Why do you think personal interaction skills are
    important to a society?

Are We Still Evolving, in a Good Way?

Many of us have been taught the theory of macroevolution, where mutations occur that allow us as a species to continue to improve and eventually get to where we are living forever, or at least a very long time, as there is no more illness. Why do we not see this happening around us?

Let's take a very simple example like eye color. Our eye color is determined by two genes, one from each parent. Brown eyes are dominant over blue eyes, so to get blue eyes, you must get blue eye genes from both parents. The genetics usually lay it out somewhat like this:

- Brown + Brown = Brown eyes
- Brown + Blue = Brown eyes
- Blue + Brown = Brown eyes
- Blue + Blue = Blue eyes

Most people who live in India and China have brown eyes, so we can assume that most of them are Brown + Brown people. But some mutations could cause some to be Brown + Blue people. Unfortunately, they would still have brown eyes. The only way to get blue-eyed Indians would be to have two mutations bump into each other and have a Blue + Blue child. The odds of forming a blue-eyed child from two Brown + Blue parents, who both are Brown + Blue people (which is rare), is one in four. However, the odds of the original mutations forming and then bumping into each other are astronomically small, hence the lack of blue-eyed Indian and Chinese people.

What about the scientific data that shows that we are slowly getting taller? This is a good example of natural selection at work within a society that is getting better healthcare and has a better diet. This is largely a technology-driven change and not a mutational change. So, it does not show good mutation changes.

Well, are there any examples of mutations within a natural selection process that are going the wrong way, making things worse? Yes, unfortunately, there are lots of them.

One simple one that we all experience each winter is the flu virus. It would seem that if we got a flu vaccine shot last year that should be good for this year, shouldn't it? Unfortunately, no because the flu virus is changing (mutating) each year. It is mutating for its own survival, and not for human convenience or survival. So, if you get a yearly flu shot, plan on getting another one, because the flu virus is mutating and it does not care anything at all for its human hosts.

What about agriculture and general foodstuffs, aren't they all getting better? Most of the agricultural changes are technology-driven to make a crop easier to harvest or perhaps more drought-resistant. These changes, along with changes to the human dietary, and biological systems have made for some interesting new developments. For example, we have been eating bread for thousands of years. It has been a mainstay not only for human substance but for human fellowship. We have been breaking bread for generations as a way of sharing our lives with others. Now, almost out of nowhere, many of us only eat gluten-free bread. Where did this come from? We would not call this a good evolutionary change as we now can no longer tolerate a most basic human sustenance, bread.

Unfortunately, the list of negative changes goes on and on. It is estimated that over 1,000 species go extinct each year. This is largely due to human interactions such as; loss of habitat, overfishing, pollution, or the introduction of a foreign, more-dominate species. Remember, extinct means dead and gone forever, never to come back again. If evolutionary changes were taking place at the rate that we were taught in school, there would be no need for concern, as new species would be forming each year at a rapid rate. Unfortunately, this does not seem to be happening. We are losing many more species than we are gaining.

Yes, evolution is still taking place, if we define it as changes or natural selection among the species; but unfortunately, it only seems to be going in the wrong direction. What does this tell us about our world going forward?

Discussion Questions

1. What do you think about the lack of blue-eyed Indians and Chinese? How might this impact your thinking about mutations for good?

2. Virus change, like the flu or the COVID-19 viruses. Do these rapid changes scare you? Why or why not?

3. Do you think that we are making food better for us, or just easier to grow? Do you think we will cross "the line" and make food irrecoverably bad for us?

4. What do you think about extinctions? Do you
    worry that one day we will wake up and see that
    it is too late? Why or why not?

What Would Charles Darwin Say About the World Today?

In the 1830s Charles Darwin embarked on a round-the-world voyage aboard the HMS Beagle ship to make scientific observations. He discovered many different animal types and behaviors that were not previously known to the European scientific community. For example, on the Galapagos islands, he observed some finches that were quite different from the common European finches. This and other observations from remote islands led him to develop the idea of microevolution.

Microevolution is the idea that changes can occur within an animal population in a localized area, and typically over a short time period (a few years to hundreds of years, instead of thousands of years). He developed the idea that these changes occurred to help the species not only survive but thrive. These changes could be from mutations or simply from natural selection. This is where we get the phrase, "The survival of the fittest."

Human societies have had almost two hundred years to internalize Darwin's ideas and use them for the greater good of the societies. So, how have we done with this?

The phrase "It is not the strongest of the species that survives, nor the most intelligent that survives. It is the one that is most adaptable to change" is often attributed to Charles Darwin.

However, we typically do not see this playing out in societies today.

Let's look at governmental systems first. Looking at many of the government leaders, we could agree that it is not the most intelligent that leads. However, we do see that the strongest are the ones that fight the hardest for survival and they also abhor change. This means that political institutions seem to be about one thing; staying in power. Individuals within a political party care foremost about their own position of power and then if they cannot increase their own power position, they care about the power position of their party. Perhaps this has not changed at all since Darwin's time or even before.

Perhaps a more modern issue is the concern about climate change. We can see that the world is changing, as Darwin would say, it always is. Perhaps it is changing faster now in some ways than it has in the past. Darwin would say that these environmental changes will bring about microevolution within the human species. Is this a good or a bad thing?

We of course do not like this idea of change. It is okay for others, but not for ourselves. Therefore, we get very passionate about some of these social issues, climate change as an example. Darwin would be surprised about our attitudes and actions for a couple of reasons.

If we believe that evolution drives everything, all changes big and small; what are we doing trying to fight it? Don't we understand that fighting evolution is a losing battle? His second concern would be a question; "If we believe that we came from a random combination of amino acids, why do we keep insisting, and with great passion, that one idea is more 'right' than another idea?" Darwin would understand that there can be no 'right' or 'wrong'; just my preferences over against your preferences. Perhaps that is why we see the great and rich crusaders for climate change all flying in their private jets to conferences on how to get others to produce less carbon dioxide. They understand Darwin's premise that the strong survive and that change is important. They understand that they will survive and they will make others change, period.

If Darwin was with us today, he would see his theory on microevolution still working in full force, but perhaps he would modify his macroevolution theory. He might agree that if we all just came from a random combination of amino acids, why should we care about anything? Is this any way to live?

Discussion Questions

1. Would Darwin still be a proponent of microevolution today? Why or why not? Give some examples.

2. What do you think about Darwin's theories when applied to world leaders, the elite, and politicians?

3. What do you think about Darwin's theory and how they are applied to climate change? What can we do?

4. How would Darwin deal with the idea of "right and wrong" today? If there is a basis for right, what would it be?

How Can We Better Harness Technology?

t is hard to define good or bad technology. In general, technology is neutral and it all comes around to how it is used.

Take, for example, nuclear energy. Nuclear power plants can produce electricity for a very long time without polluting the atmosphere with carbon dioxide and other by-products that come from coal-fired power plants. However, nuclear power plants are not totally clean as they have their own problem of disposing of spent nuclear fuel, which lasts a really long time. Of course, there can be horrible disasters, such as what happened in Chernobyl, Russia. Yet, almost 20% of the electrical power in the US is made from nuclear power plants.

When the Apple iPhone was launched in 2007, it was not the first smartphone. It was not the first device that played music, took photos, or had a web browser. However, it was the first device that did all of these things smoothly and simply. Was the iPhone great technology? No question. However, is smartphone technology all for good? Given the rise of loneliness among young adults, its goodness could be debated.

How could we better determine if early new technology is good for us and how can we put boundaries around its use?

The Amish people are viewed to be anti-technology, but that is not totally true. There are different uses of technology in different Amish communities. But, many of them use the same test for new technology. They will bring a new technology into the community for use by just a few members. These members will use the technology for a limited time, say a few months. At the end of this time, the entire community assembles to discuss the merits of the new technology, with a particular focus on the benefit for the community, not the individual. This focus on the entire community is a different approach than most Western, technological societies.

An example of the Amish approach is the use of gasoline tractors by some Amish and Mennonites. They decided that the tractor was a useful piece of farm equipment. The tractor could plow, harvest, and haul more effectively than a pair of horses. However, the Amish did not want the tractor to be used as transportation between communities, especially on asphalt roads. Therefore, they replaced the rubber tires with steel tires. The steel tires work well in the fields, but they do not work well on asphalt roads. On asphalt, they produce a very uncomfortable ride between communities. However, the tractor provides a great benefit to the community in terms of planting and harvesting. But, as a method of transportation between communities, it is a poor substitute for the horse and buggy. The buggy can carry many more people. It does not use expensive gasoline for fuel. It does not produce air pollution, and it does allow for community discussion during the journey.

Perhaps the Amish thought that Matthew, in the New Testament, expected the community to gather together face-to-face and not electronically or on social media:

> *19 "Again I say to you that if two of you agree on earth concerning anything that they ask, it will be done for them by My Father in heaven. 20 For where two or three are gathered together in My name, I am there in the midst of them." (Matthew 18:19-20)*

Much of the time today, the technology discussion is focused on the benefit for the individual. Perhaps we all would be better off if we thought about technology beyond ourselves, beyond making money, and more about building community, when two or three of us gather together.

Photo credit: Reba Tyrrell

Discussion Questions

1. What do you think about this community view of technology? Are there any drawbacks to this community-view approach?

2. Can you think about how smartphone
    technology could be used for community
    building?

3. What drawback would there be to limiting the
    technology to a community-focus only?

4. What would it take for you to give up your
    personal smartphone?

Why Don't Toilets Clean Themselves?

Life would be so much better if we did not have to do all of the annoying tasks, but unfortunately, it is not meant to be.

In the 1800s the fundamental laws of thermodynamics came to be understood and codified. Simply stated the first law says the heat always goes from the hotter to the colder, and never from the colder to the hotter. The second law states that entropy; chaos, or disorder, is always increasing. The third law says that eventually, the universe will suffer a heat death with everything at the same, very, very cold temperature. There appears to be no way around these three laws.

Perhaps that is why, at the beginning of time, God gave humankind the task of taking care of the world.

Then God blessed them, and God said to them, "Be fruitful and multiply; fill the earth and subdue it; have dominion over the fish of the sea, over the birds of the air, and over every living thing that moves on the earth." (Genesis 1:28)

Dominion is a way of caring for the creation. But, alas, it is a hard task, especially given the population explosion that came with the Industrial Revolution.

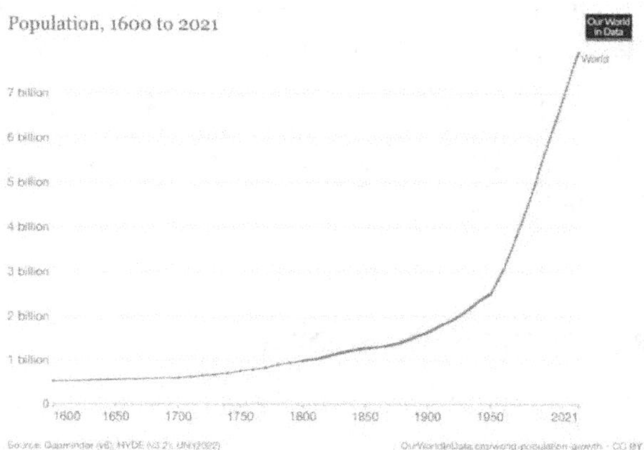

As you can see the world's population was about 1 billion in 1900, and 2 billion in 1950. Now we are approaching 8 billion and there seems to be no end in sight.

People need to be taken care of, and there are lots of tasks that are a pain to do, like cleaning your toilet. Some hope that artificial intelligence, AI, and the robot revolution will take care of many of these mundane tasks, but even with those technological advances, there will still be tasks that need to be done by people.

After all, we are very good at giving empathetic, loving care when we apply ourselves. Sometimes these tasks are inconvenient and a pain, but they need to be done. When they are done with the right attitude, they even bring us a surprising amount of joy. Being connected to others is one of the most important aspects of a fulfilling life. So, the next time you are clearing a toilet or doing some other mundane task think of it as a way of serving others. Perhaps you will begin to see:

Then God saw everything that He had made, and indeed it was very good. (Genesis 1:31

Discussion Questions

1. Do you think our lives are better and more fulfilled than your grandparents? Why or why not?

2. What do you think about the world's population growth? Are destined to kill ourselves with overpopulation? Why or why not?

3. What do you think about having a personal robot in your home to do the mundane tasks, like cleaning your toilet?

4. Can you think of a time when you got great joy doing a simple, serving task? Describe why it brought such joy.

Why Should I Even Care?

Our worldview has a lot to say about why we should even care. If someone has the worldview that the universe "exploded into being" with the Big Bang, it is tough to come up with a reason to care. Exploding into being does not bring with it any care, compassion, reason for personal relationships, or any purpose or value in our work.

If we skip over the origin of the Big Bang and move to evolutionary Darwinism, we see a world of amino acids struggling to survive and somehow overcoming the other amino acid entities. There is no reason why one bunch of amino acids should be better, more important, or more valuable than another bunch. Unfortunately, it usually comes down to the idea that my batch of amino acids are more important than yours, so I will fight for mine.

When this evolutionary Darwinism view does not seem to work for us, we often look to thinkers like Jean-Paul Sartre and his existentialism as a way to make sense of all that is. Satre did not know where we came from or why, but he still posited that we should still try to find some purpose in life. Confusingly, he said that there is no objective right or wrong, and there is no real way to find true meaning, so we should just decide on our own and make our own meaning. We must find our own purpose, and not let others judge our view of the meaning of life. We are all born without reason, we live a life filled with weakness, and then we die by chance. Life is a useless passion, yet we still feel that we need to make something of it.

Why is this?

Why do we try to make connections with people, causes, and projects? Why do we not like the feeling of loneliness? Why do we try to engage with other people, why do we enjoy sharing our lives with others, and why do we sometimes do nice things for others? Why do we engage in personal development projects like, weight loss, learning a new skill, or reaching out to new people who might become friends? If life is a useless passion, it makes no sense; and yet we try to make our lives better. Why do we do this?

Perhaps this most strongly points to an Intelligent Designer behind all that is. We see this in the beginning with the Biblical Creation narrative, where we find our place in the world.

> *27 So God created man in His own image; in the image of God He created him; male and female He created them. 28 Then God blessed them, and God said to them, "Be fruitful and multiply; fill the earth and subdue it; have dominion over the fish of the sea, over the birds of the air, and over every living thing that moves on the earth." (Genesis 1:27-28)*

We are made in the image of the Creator. He has given us intelligence, the ability to love, create, make art, and the will to do better. He gives us a job to do, to take care of the earth. He gives us a reason to be here and a reason to care.

Is there any other reason to care?

Discussion Questions

1. Can you come up with a reason to care if you believe that all that is just "exploded into being"? How would you explain this to someone else?

2. What is wrong with Darwin's view of the survival of the fittest? Can I be happy if I just look out for "Number One", that is myself?

3. Some find that Sartre's view that life is a useless passion is crazy. But, if we are all just a cosmic accident, what is wrong with this view?

4. How would you explain the idea of an Intelligent
    Designer to a non-believer in this view?

5. Does the Intelligent Designer view give us a
    reason to care or not?

Concluding Thoughts

Understanding the world and our place in it can be hard. Sometimes it is hard to know what to do. Other times we know what we should do, but we do not want to do it.

Every generation thinks that there are parts of their society that are messed up. Do you think there are answers to some of these big, societal questions? How could you go about making big or small changes to your world?

Hopefully, some of these reflections helped you to understand more about how to think about these big-picture questions and life in general.

Perhaps it is time to get together with some friends and talk about these issues and what you can do.

TS Taylor

Prayer to Accept Jesus

If you found this reflections book helpful and you felt God tugging at your heart. If you came to see that God does exist and that He wants to have a personal relationship with you, you can respond to the Holy Spirit right now.

If you have never accepted Jesus as your own personal Lord and Savior, you can do that with a simple prayer.

You can pray something like this:

"Thank you, God, for loving me and sending your Son to die for my sins. I sincerely repent of my sins, and receive Christ as my personal savior. Now, as your child, I turn my entire life over to you. Amen."

If you have any questions, you can reach out to me at:

tstaylor.devotionals@gmail.com

May God bless you on your own spiritual journey.

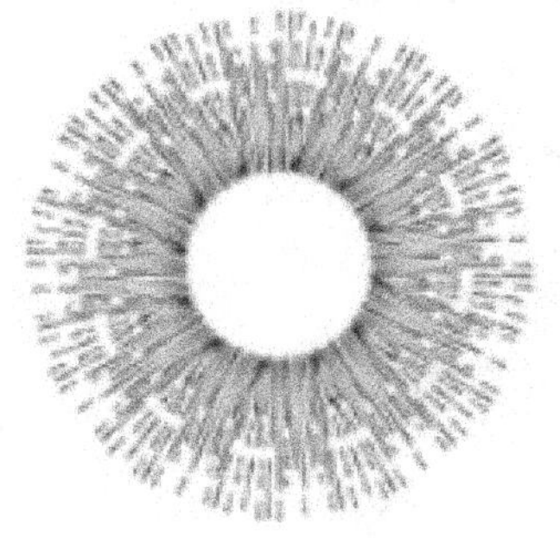

Acknowledgments

I wish to thank my class at the Church of the Apostles in Atlanta, Georgia. They worked through much of this material, as we learned from the Scriptures together.

Soli Deo Gloria

www.ingramcontent.com/pod-product-compliance
Lightning Source LLC
Chambersburg PA
CBHW050800160726
48004CB00002B/647